Khalil Gibran poems
Major scale
Music Atherma C#
Simple Tetraktys
Disyllable Iamb

By Gregory Zorzos

Gregory Zorzos, a native Hellene, was born in Kallithea, Athens in Greece (Hellas) at 1958. Author and his research work have been distinguished by a lot of official organizations, and Ministries, in Greece and all over the world. The author has wrote and published more than 3,500,000 works (books, board games, DVDs, CD-Roms, DVD-Roms, audio CDs, MP3s, E-books, E-pubs, MP4s etc) about ancient and modern history in the fields of economics, technical, board games, martial arts, software, love affairs, feasibilities studies, research, case studies, learning languages, logodynamics, inner research etc. Many awards and credits around the world. As a reporter, from his teens, the author has written many articles in many newspapers, magazines etc and was editor in chief in some of them. Researches have been approved or accepted from the Ministry of Education, Ministry of Culture, Hellenic Army, Ministry of Foreign Affairs, Group Unesco Piraeus and Islands, SAE, etc. Works have been register in Copyright Offices in Greece, USA and Canada.

Gregory Zorzos [Greece]

Khalil Gibran poems

Major scale

Music Atherma C# – Simple Tetraktys * Disyllable Iamb

Gregory Zorzos

Author Director Composer

Gregory Zorzos [Greece]

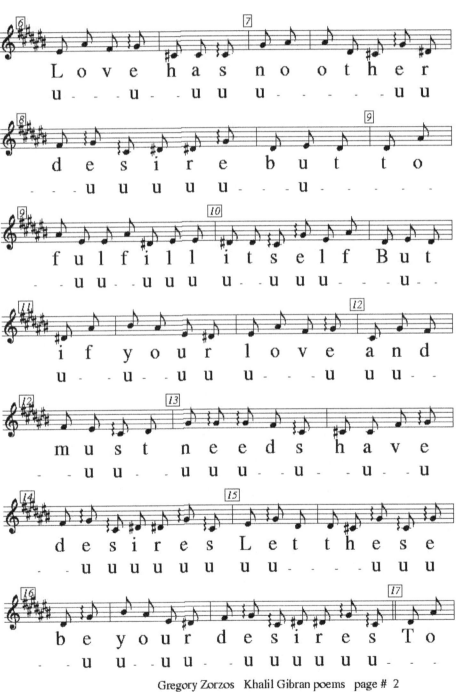

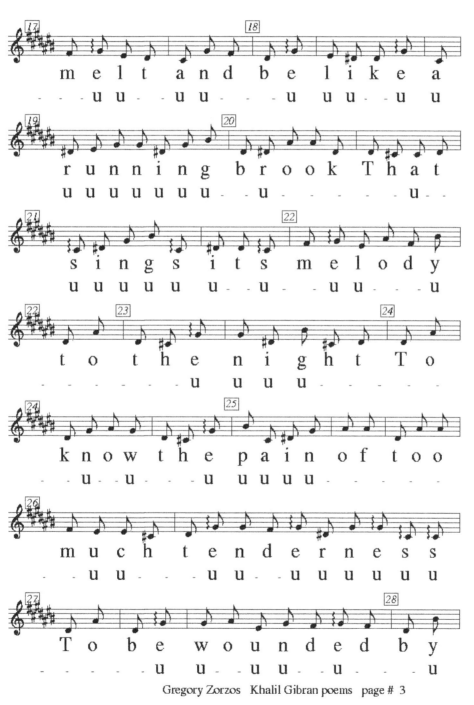

Gregory Zorzos [Greece]

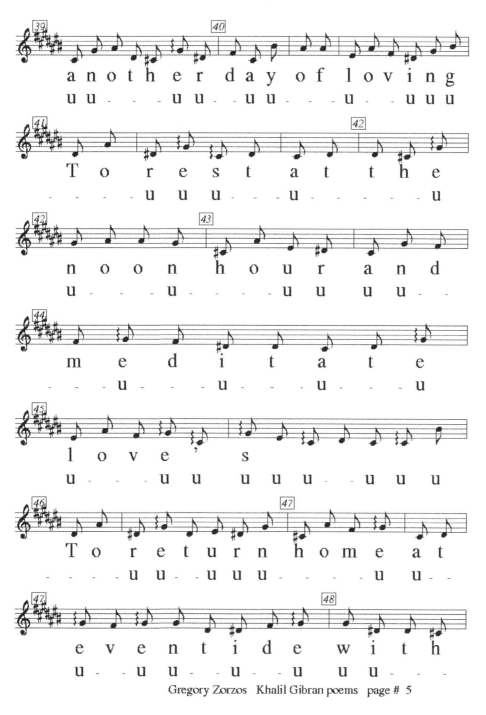

Gregory Zorzos [Greece]

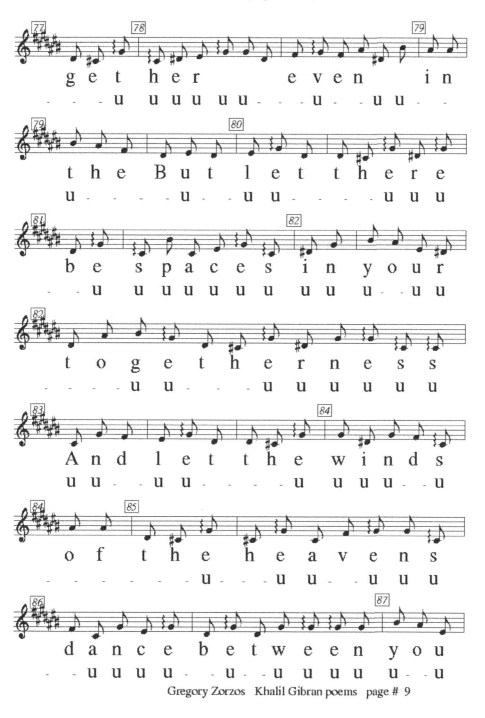

Gregory Zorzos [Greece]

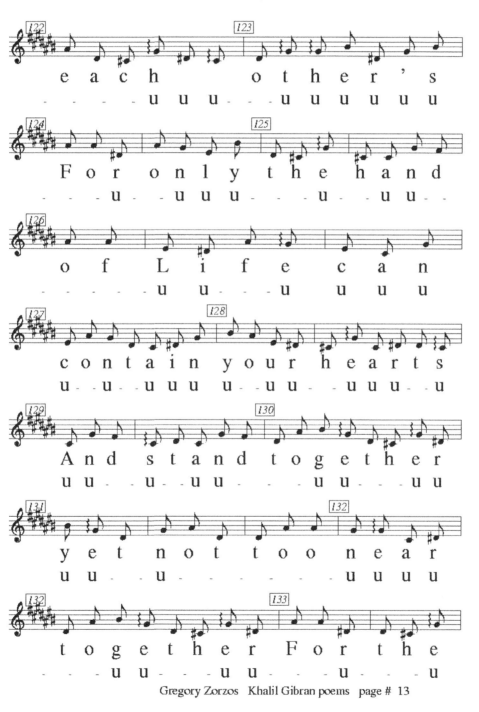

Gregory Zorzos [Greece]

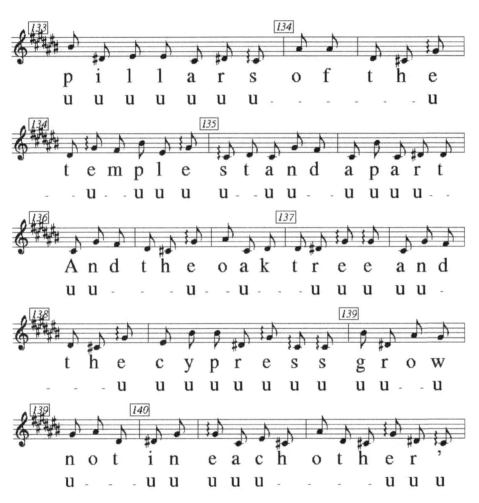

Gregory Zorzos [Greece]

S

u - - u - - u

Created at Athens [Greece] by Gregory Zorzos
Gregory Zorzos
Author Director Composer
with Major scale
Metre and Rhythm Simple Tetraktys * Disyllable Iamb
Ancient Greek Pythagorean music
− = long syllable, u = short syllable (macron and breve notation)

Gregory Zorzos [Greece]

Khalil Gibran poems

Major scale

Music Atherma B – Simple Tetraktys * Disyllable Iamb

Gregory Zorzos

Author Director Composer

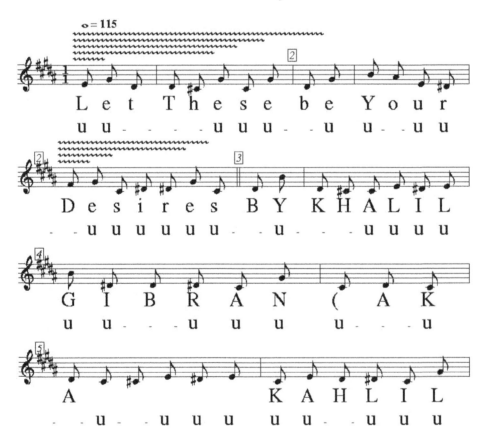

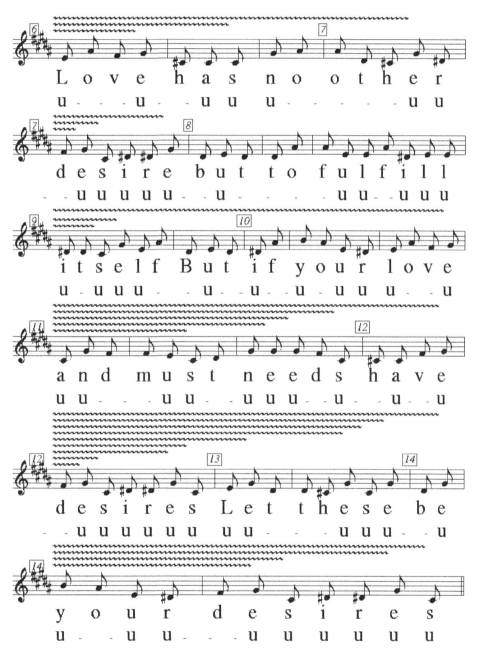

Gregory Zorzos [Greece]

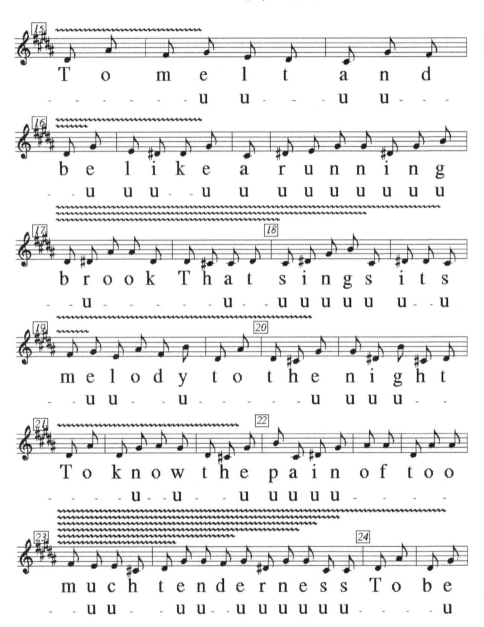

Gregory Zorzos [Greece]

Gregory Zorzos [Greece]

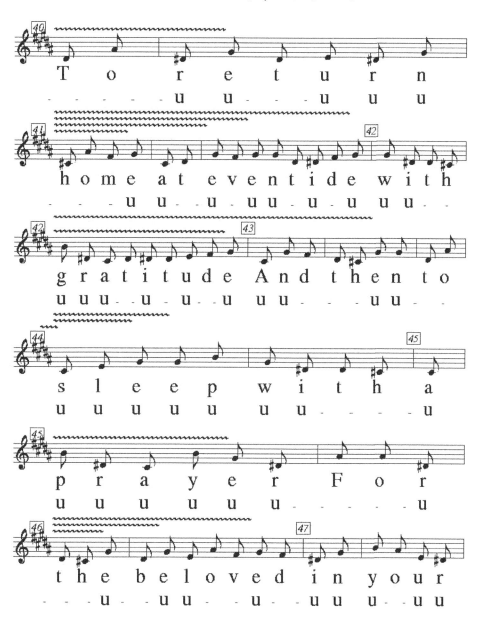

Gregory Zorzos [Greece]

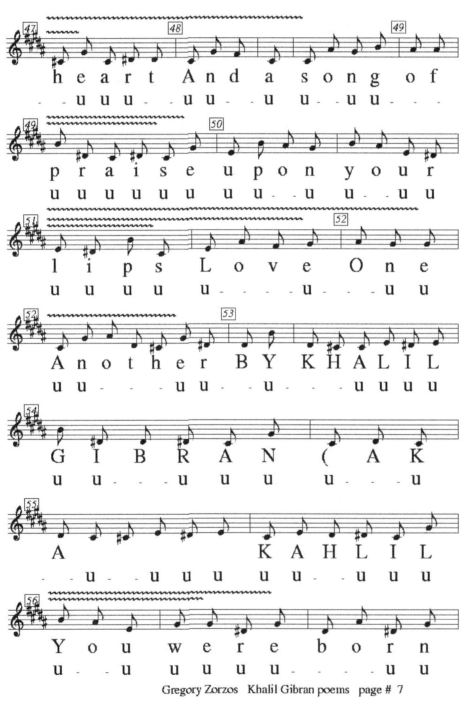

Gregory Zorzos [Greece]

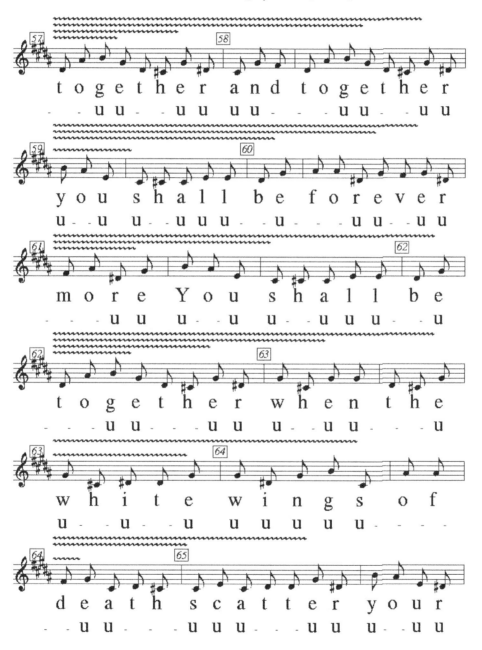

Gregory Zorzos [Greece]

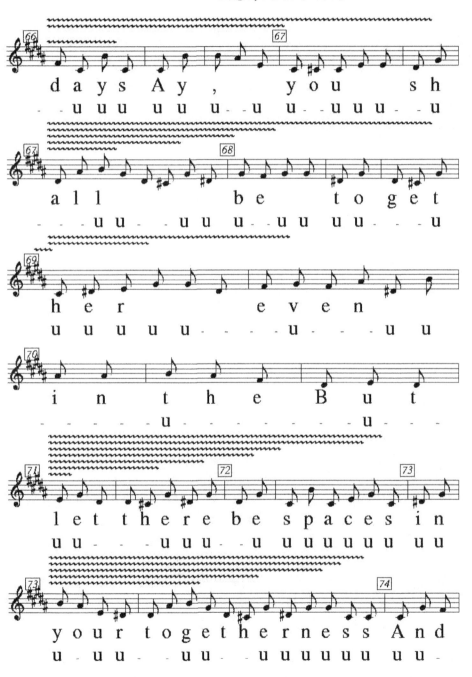

Gregory Zorzos [Greece]

Gregory Zorzos [Greece]

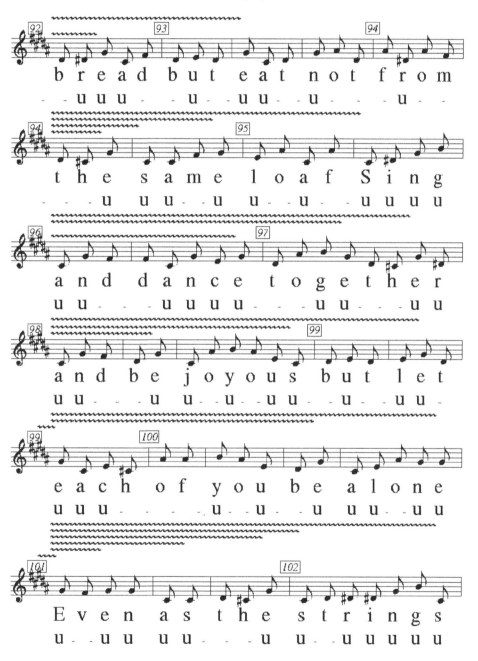

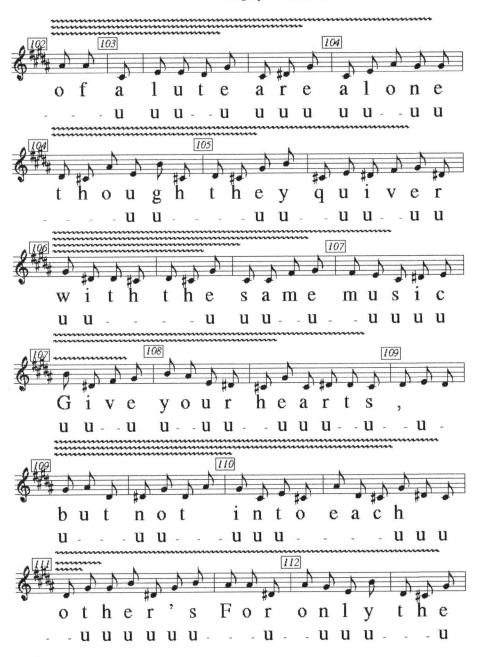

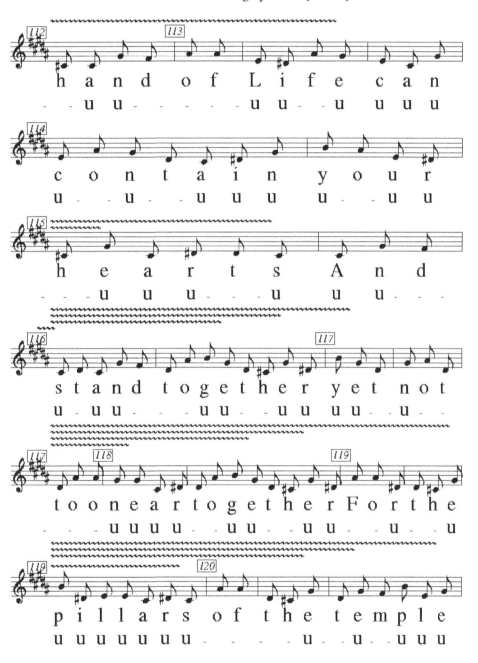

Gregory Zorzos [Greece]

Created at Athens [Greece] by Gregory Zorzos
Gregory Zorzos
Author Director Composer
with Major scale
Metre and Rhythm Simple Tetraktys * Disyllable Iamb
Ancient Greek Pythagorean music
− = long syllable, u = short syllable (macron and breve notation)

Gregory Zorzos [Greece]

Khalil Gibran poems

Major scale

Music Atherma A – Simple Tetraktys * Disyllable Iamb

Gregory Zorzos

Author Director Composer

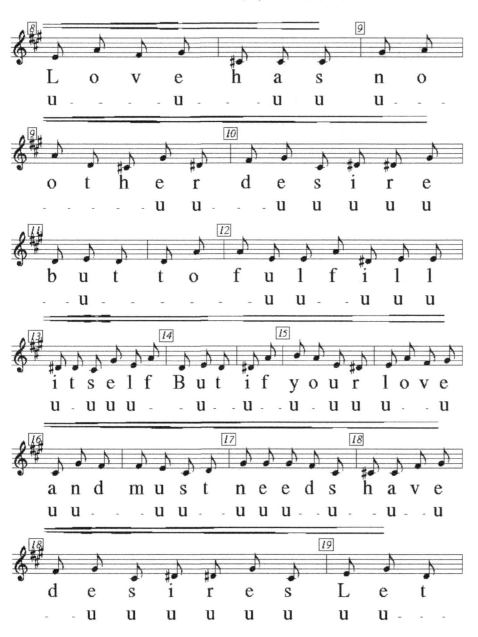

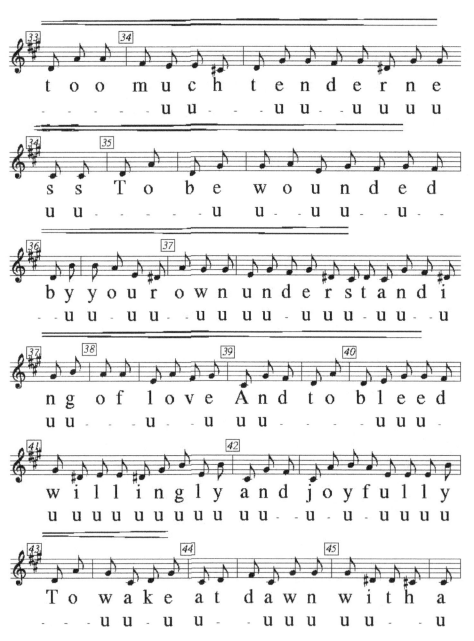

Gregory Zorzos [Greece]

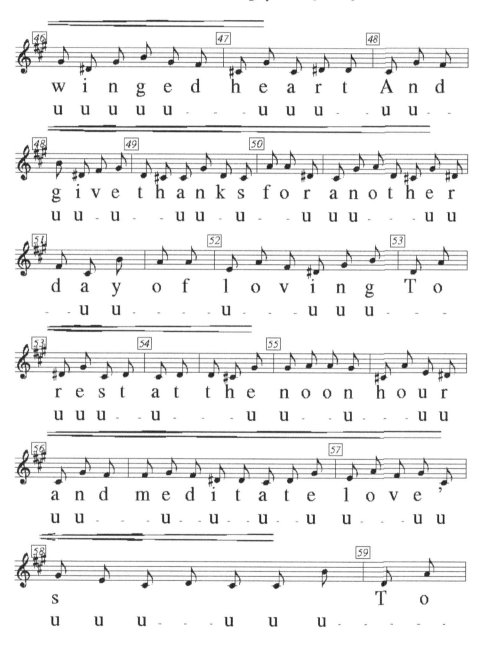

Gregory Zorzos [Greece]

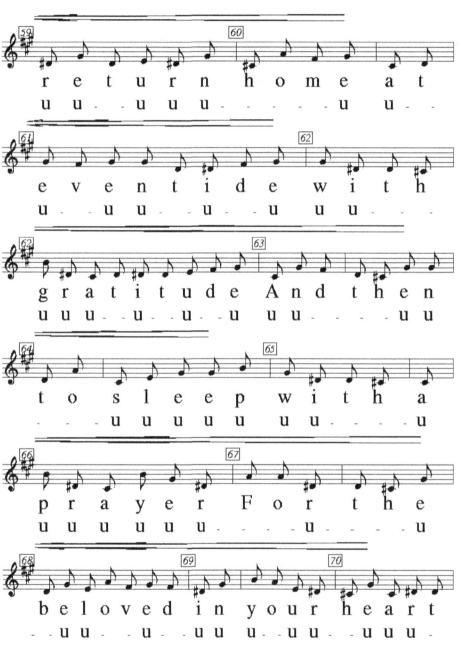

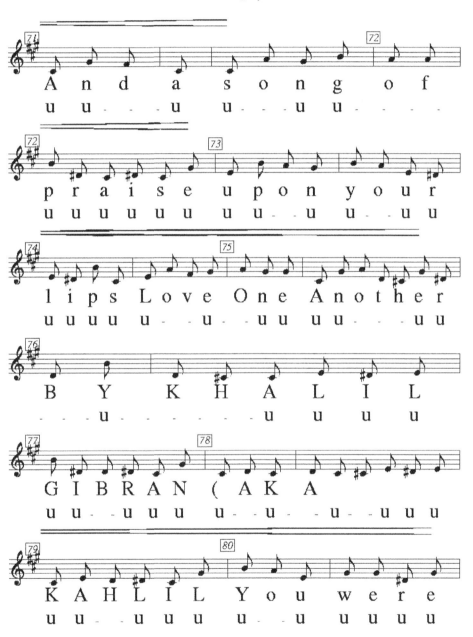

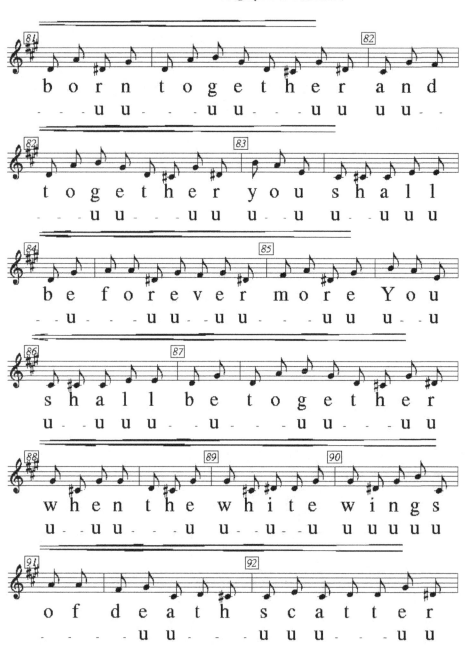

Gregory Zorzos [Greece]

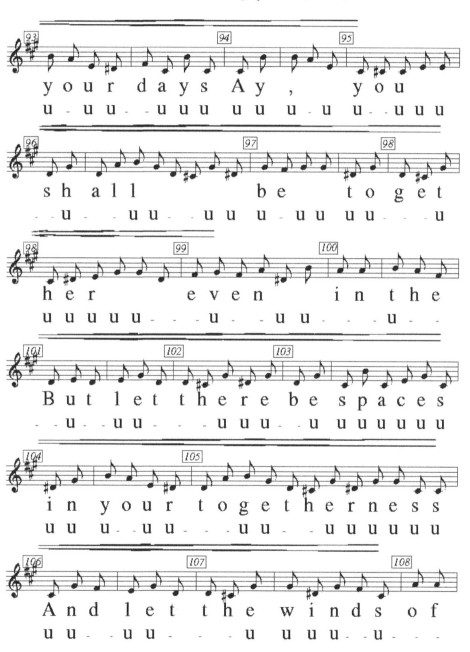

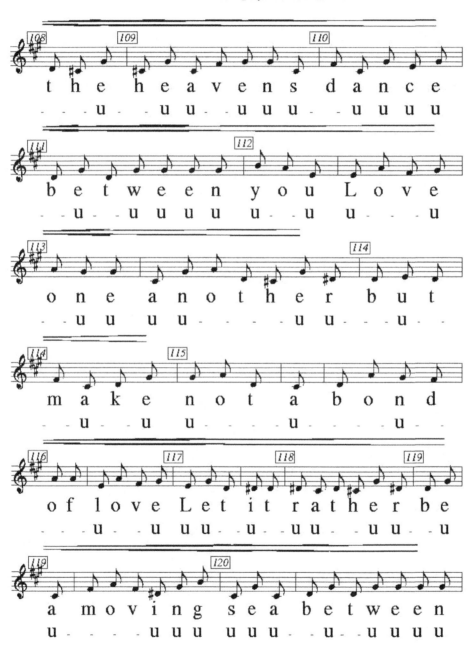

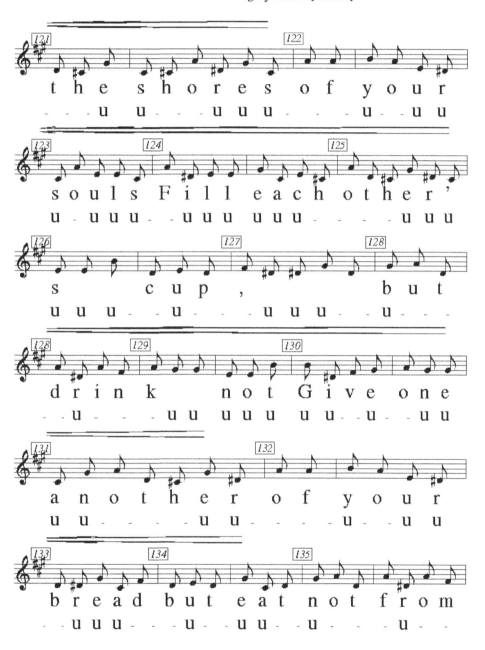

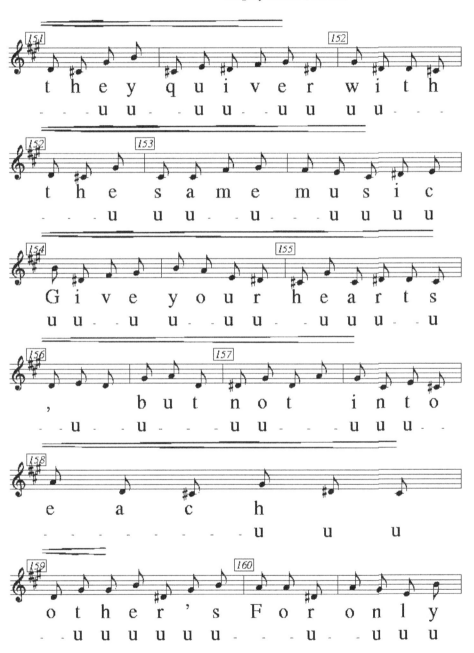

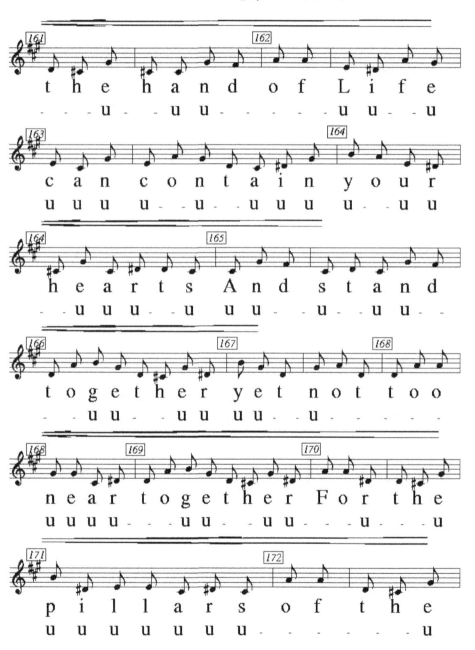

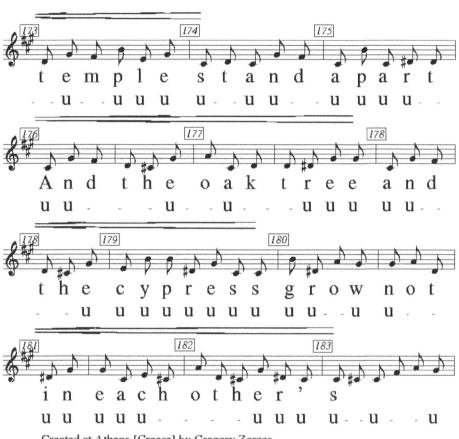

temple stand apart
- u - - u u u u - u u - u u u u -

And the oak tree and
u u - - - u - - u - - u u u u u u -

the cypress grow not
- - u u u u u u u u - u u - - u u - -

in each other's
u u - u u u - - - - u u u u - u - - u

Created at Athens [Greece] by Gregory Zorzos
Gregory Zorzos
Author Director Composer
with Major scale
Metre and Rhythm Simple Tetraktys * Disyllable Iamb
Ancient Greek Pythagorean music
– = long syllable, u = short syllable (macron and breve notation)

Gregory Zorzos [Greece]

Khalil Gibran poems

Major scale

Music Atherma G – Simple Tetraktys * Disyllable Iamb

Gregory Zorzos

Author Director Composer

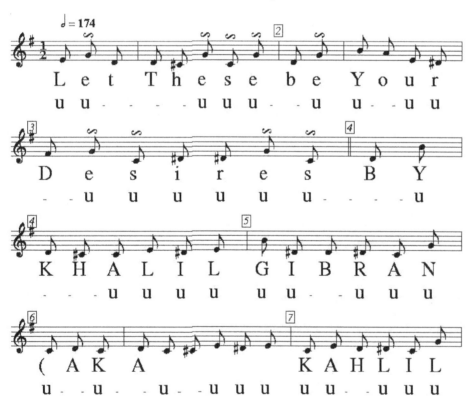

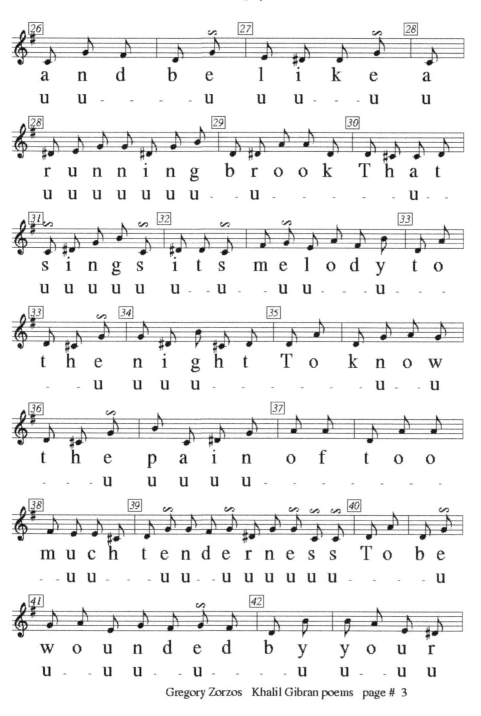

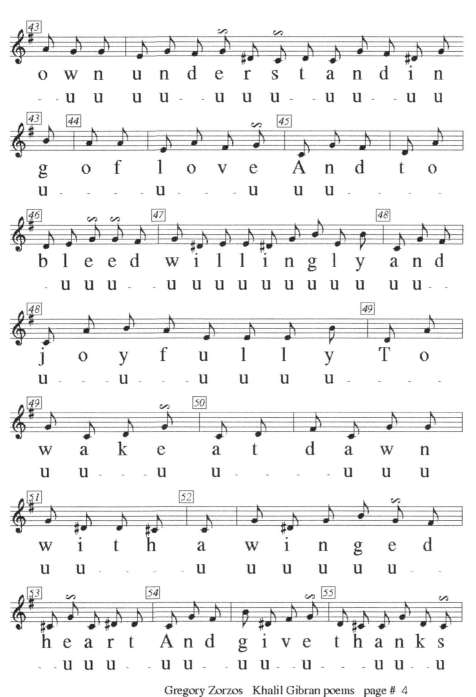

Gregory Zorzos [Greece]

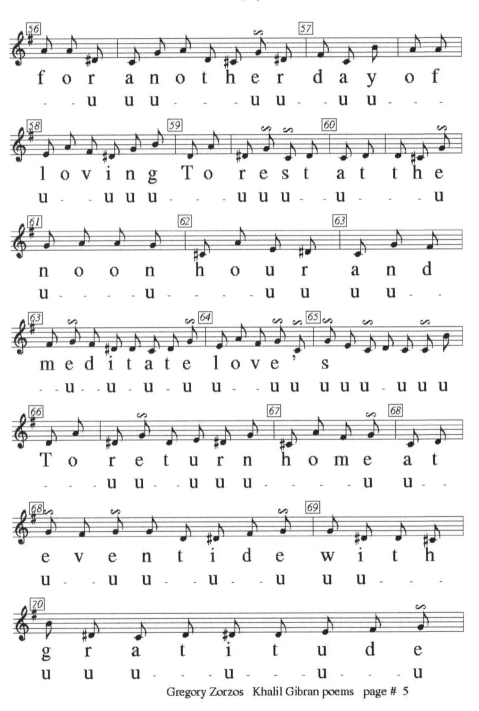

for another day of
- - u u u - - - u u u - u u - -

loving To rest at the
u - - u u u - - u u u - u - - u

noon hour and
u - - - u - - - u u u u -

meditate love's
- - u - u - u - u u - u u u u u - u u u

To return home at
- - - u u - - u u u - - u u -

eventide with
u - - u u - u - u - u u u - - -

gratitude
u u u - - - u - - - u - - - u

Gregory Zorzos   Khalil Gibran poems   page # 5

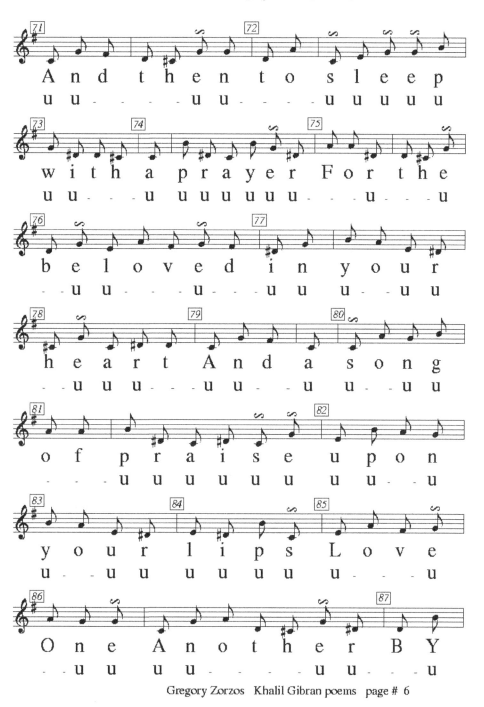

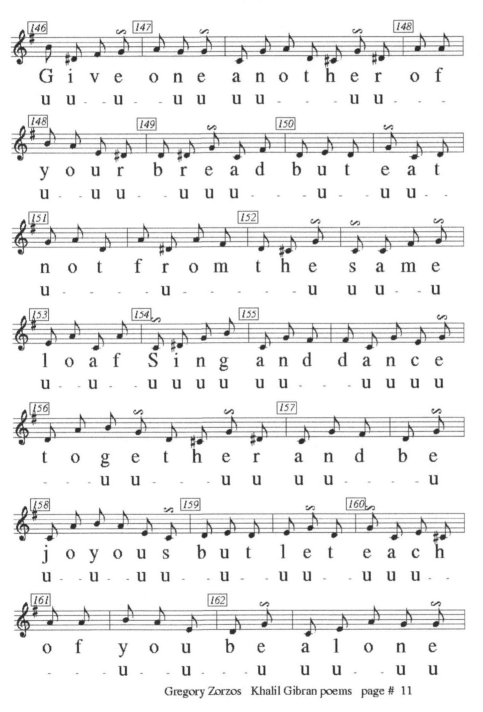

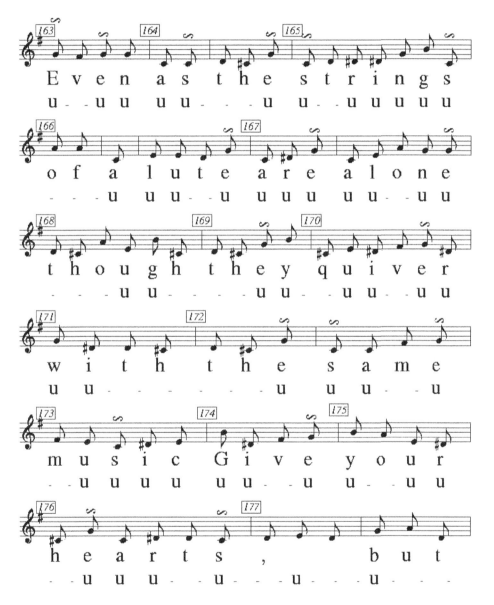

Gregory Zorzos [Greece]

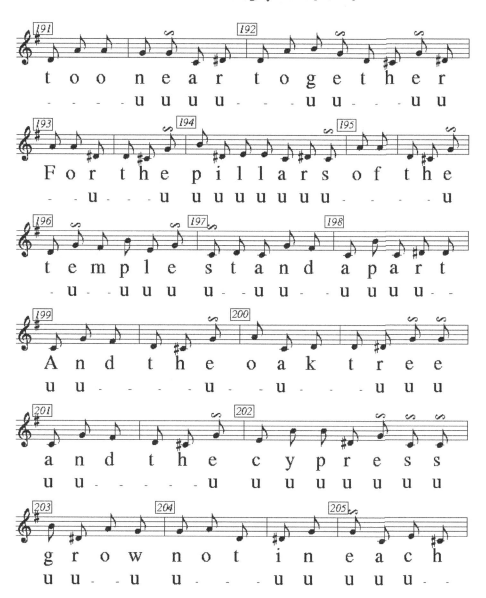

Gregory Zorzos [Greece]

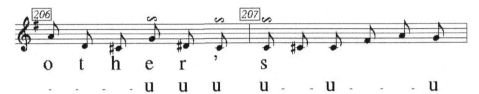

o t h e r ' s

- - - - u u u u - u - - - u

Created at Athens [Greece] by Gregory Zorzos
Gregory Zorzos
Author Director Composer
with Major scale
Metre and Rhythm Simple Tetraktys * Disyllable Iamb
Ancient Greek Pythagorean music
− = long syllable, u = short syllable (macron and breve notation)

Gregory Zorzos [Greece]

Khalil Gibran poems

Major scale

Music Atherma F – Simple Tetraktys * Disyllable Iamb

Gregory Zorzos

Author Director Composer

Gregory Zorzos [Greece]

Gregory Zorzos [Greece]

Gregory Zorzos [Greece]

Gregory Zorzos [Greece]

Gregory Zorzos [Greece]

Gregory Zorzos [Greece]

Gregory Zorzos [Greece]

Gregory Zorzos [Greece]

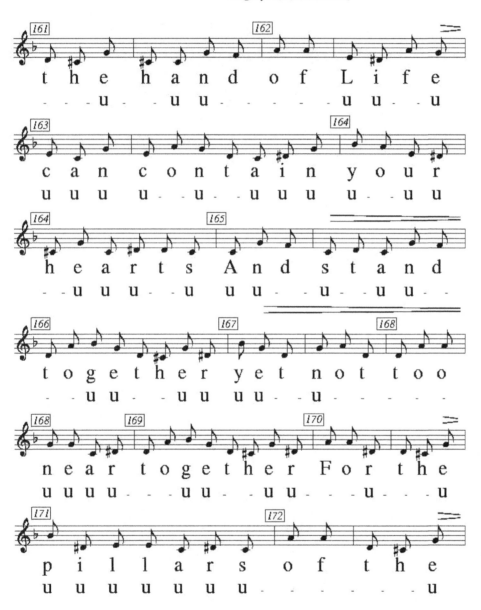

Gregory Zorzos [Greece]

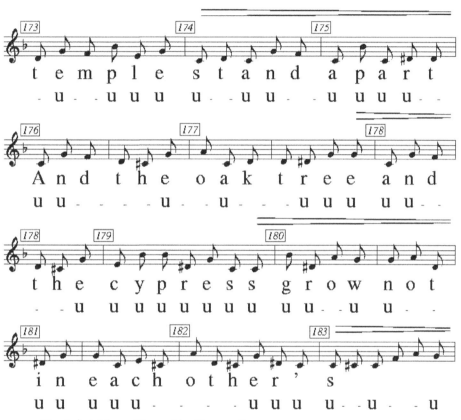

Created at Athens [Greece] by Gregory Zorzos
Gregory Zorzos
Author Director Composer
with Major scale
Metre and Rhythm Simple Tetraktys * Disyllable Iamb
Ancient Greek Pythagorean music
– = long syllable, u = short syllable (macron and breve notation)

Made in the USA
Middletown, DE
07 June 2021